TAILS from History

A Raccoon at the White House

By Rachel Dougherty

Illustrated by Rachel Sanson

Ready-to-Read

Simon Spotlight

New York London Toronto Sydney New Delhi

Dedicated to Laurie and to my critique group for
helping this story grow and finding it a home —R. D.

For my dad —R. S.

SIMON SPOTLIGHT
An imprint of Simon & Schuster Children's Publishing Division
1230 Avenue of the Americas, New York, New York 10020
This Simon Spotlight edition July 2018
Text copyright © 2018 by Rachel Dougherty
Illustrations copyright © 2018 by Rachel Sanson
For information about special discounts for bulk purchases, please contact Simon & Schuster Special
Sales at 1-866-506-1949 or business@simonandschuster.com.
Manufactured in the United States of America 0918 LAK
10 9 8 7 6 5 4 3 2
Library of Congress Cataloging-in-Publication Data
Names: Dougherty, Rachel, 1988- author. | Sanson, Rachel, illustrator. Title: A raccoon at the White
House / by Rachel Dougherty ; illustrated by Rachel Sanson. Description: First Simon Spotlight
hardcover/paperback edition. | New York : Simon Spotlight, 2018. | Series: Tails from history | Series:
Ready-to-read | Audience: Age 5-7. Identifiers: LCCN 2017054383 | ISBN 9781534405424 (hardcover) |
ISBN 9781534405417 (paperback) | ISBN 9781534405431 (ebook) Subjects: LCSH: Coolidge, Calvin,
1872-1933—Juvenile literature. | Raccoons as pets—Washington (D.C.)—Anecdotes—Juvenile literature.
Classification: LCC SF459.R22 D68 2018 | DDC 636.976/32—dc23
LC record available at https://lccn.loc.gov/2017054383

The year was 1926.
Nestled in paper, a critter peeked out of her box.
Shiny shoes walked toward her.

Suddenly the box top swung open.
The President and First Lady
looked down and gasped.
They were very surprised
to find a raccoon!

The First Lady frowned,
peeking into the box.
"A raccoon to eat for Thanksgiving
dinner?" she yelped.
"Not for us! We'll keep her!"

And they called her Rebecca.

Rebecca was in good company
at the White House.
President Calvin Coolidge
and his wife, Grace, loved pets.
There were so many birds
and cats and dogs.

One of the cats, Tiger,
liked to be worn as a scarf.

Knowing the Coolidges
loved all animals,
foreign leaders sent pets as gifts.
Calvin welcomed them all.

There were lion cubs
from South Africa
and thirteen Pekin ducklings!
Still, Rebecca was special.

Calvin and Grace built Rebecca
a tree house,
but she ate most of her meals
with the family.

Rebecca ate chicken, shrimp, and a type of fruit called persimmons (say: per-SIM-mons). But she liked eggs the most!

At the White House Easter Egg Roll,
Rebecca couldn't understand why
everyone chased the eggs
instead of eating them.

Rebecca loved Calvin and Grace.
Their donkey, Ebenezer, did too.

Rebecca was always waiting
for Calvin to finish his work.
He was the only one who liked
to play with her.
She tried to play with Old Bill,
Calvin's pet bird.
But Old Bill was not interested.

The wallaby from Tasmania
hopped up and down the stairs.
But raccoons aren't
made for hopping.

Calvin's bobcat, Smoky,
or the big black bear
from Mexico
might have been
Rebecca's friends . . .

but they were
never home.

Neither was Calvin's pygmy hippo,
who Calvin said swam all day
in a pond across town.

Rebecca swam in her tub all alone.

So Rebecca had to make her own fun.

She tore up
sheets,

got into
the garbage,

and chewed
on all the
President's
shoes.

"Shame on you!" scolded Grace.
"Beastly!" cried Calvin.

For the first time, the staff at the White House was grumpy. They loved the dogs and cats. They whistled with the birds.

But Rebecca did not fit in.

Sometimes Rebecca disappeared.
Calvin and Grace would find her
at the edges of the property.

Calvin and Grace knew
Rebecca needed a new home
with other raccoons.

They took her uptown
to a place as special as she was.

There were sticks to chew on!
There were rocks to scratch!
Rebecca chased and tumbled
and wrestled all day.
She loved her new raccoon friends.

Grace and Calvin were relieved.
And they were glad they lived
so close to the National Zoo!

· Facts About Raccoons ·

• On average, raccoons are 2-3 feet long and weigh between 14 and 23 pounds.

• Wild raccoons usually live about 2-3 years, but in captivity, they can live up to 20 years.

• Raccoons eat almost anything they can find, including fruits, plants, nuts, berries, insects, frogs, and eggs. In cities, raccoons usually scavenge in the garbage for food.

• Baby raccoons are called kits, and a group of raccoons is called a gaze.

• As cute as they look, raccoons do not usually make good pets because of their mischievous nature. If you see one in your neighborhood, do not go near it. They are wild animals who love to scratch and bite, and they don't like to be contained.

· Facts About the White House ·

• Theodore Roosevelt was the first to officially call the president's home the White House in 1901.

• These days, the White House has 132 rooms, including a movie theater and a bowling alley.

• There is a twin White House in Ireland called the Leinster House. Its design influenced the work of the White House's architect, James Hoban, who was born in Ireland.

• George Washington never lived in the White House. He is the only president who did not.

• The White House sits on a park of 18 acres of land. That's the size of about 13 football fields.

While the Coolidges certainly had all the pets mentioned in this book, they may not have all lived in the White House at the same time. However, Rebecca's stay at the White House probably overlapped with many of these animals.